*Golden Crow*

# Táhirih

*by*

## Lowell Johnson

The National Spiritual Assembly
of the Bahá'ís of South and West Africa

*Johannesburg*

ISBN 0 908420 29 3

# Introduction to the *Golden Crowns* Series

In these next pages you will read of great sacrifices. Anyone reading the stories of the early believers in the Bahá'í Faith will wonder why these people sacrificed so much. What was different about the Messages of the Báb and Bahá'u'lláh which made ordinary people rise to the heights of heroism and die gloriously for their Faith?

The teachings of the Báb* and Bahá'u'lláh† repeat the divine principles announced by the Prophets of the past. You can read these teachings in a very small book entitled *The Hidden Words*. It was written by Bahá'u'lláh. But added to these eternal truths, the Báb and Bahá'u'lláh have given new teachings never announced by any Prophet of God before. Here are some of them:

The first teaching of the Bahá'í Faith is that all men belong to one human family. Speaking to all men, Bahá'u'lláh says, 'Ye are the fruits of one tree and the leaves of one branch.' By this He means that the world of men is like a tree, the nations and peoples are the different branches of that tree, and the men and women are as the fruits and blossoms of that tree. In all past religions, the world of men was divided into two parts—one part known as the people of the Book of God or the pure tree, and the other known as the lost people or the evil tree. Bahá'u'lláh has changed this teaching by announcing that the world is one world and all people in it members of one family. This is a special teaching of Bahá'u'lláh not to be found in any other religion. Some people are asleep, He says, and they need to be awakened; some are sick, they need to be healed; some are like children, they need to be taught; but all receive the bounty and gifts of God.

* The Báb is the title given to the Forerunner of Bahá'u'lláh. He was born in Shíráz, Írán (Persia) on the 20th of October 1819 and was martyred in Tabríz, Írán, on the 9th of July 1850. The 'Báb' means the 'Gate'.

† Bahá'u'lláh is the name of God's newest Manifestation on earth. He was born in Ṭihrán, Írán on the 12th of November 1817 and died near Haifa, Israel on the 29th of May 1892. 'Bahá'u'lláh' means the 'Glory of God'.

Another new principle in the Bahá'í Faith is the need to investigate truth. That is to say, no man should blindly follow his ancestors and forefathers. Each man must see with his own eyes, hear with his own ears, and investigate truth for himself.

Another teaching is this: that the foundation of all the religions of God is one. There is only one God. Therefore, there can be only one religion—the Religion of God. All the past Prophets have taught the same basic truths, which have all come from the same mouth of God. This teaching is a new teaching and is special in the Bahá'í Faith.

A new principle is that religion must be the cause of unity, harmony and agreement amongst men. If religion becomes the cause of disagreement and hatred, if it leads to separation and fighting, then it would be better if there were no religion in the world.

The Bahá'í Faith also teaches that religion must agree with science and reason. If it does not agree with science and reason then it is superstition. Down to the present day it has been the custom for a man to accept a religious teaching even if it does not agree with his reason and judgement. The agreement of religious belief with reason and science opens new windows to the soul of man.

Bahá'u'lláh has taught the equality of men and women. This is special to the teachings of the Bahá'í Faith, for all other religions have placed men above women.

A new religious principle is that prejudices, whether religious, racial, patriotic or political, destroy the solid foundation for a peaceful life. Therefore, men must overcome their prejudices so that they can see the underlying truth, that the family of man is one family and not divided into separate parts.

Universal peace is promised in the Bahá'í teachings. This universal peace will be accomplished by putting into practice the principles of Bahá'u'lláh. Peace shall come to all nations, governments, peoples, religions, races, and all parts of mankind. No other Prophet has ever promised peace to the world during His ministry, but this is one of the special teachings of Bahá'u'lláh.

The Báb and Bahá'u'lláh have taught that every man must gain knowledge and receive an education. It is a religious law in the Bahá'í Faith that both girls and boys must be educated.

Bahá'u'lláh has set forth the solution and provided the remedy for the economic question. The solution of the economic problem, He says, lies in the realm of the spirit. No religious books of the past Prophets speak of this important human problem.

The greatest new principle of the new religion is the establishment and appointment of the Centre of the Covenant. This is another teaching not given by any of the Prophets of the past. Bahá'u'lláh has appointed a Centre of the Covenant* to carry on His work and hold the Bahá'ís together after His passing. When a person becomes a Bahá'í, he must agree to follow the laws contained in the Covenant. In this way, Bahá'u'lláh has protected the religion of God against differences and splits. He has made it impossible for anyone to create a new sect or faction of belief. To make sure of the unity of the believers, He has entered into a Covenant with all the people of the world, including the Interpreter and Explainer of His teachings, so that no one may interpret or explain the religion of God according to his own ideas or opinion, and thus create a sect founded upon his own understanding of the divine words.

These are some of the principles of religion brought by the Báb and Bahá'u'lláh which are different from the religions of the past. Thousands of men and women died during the nineteenth century rather than give up their faith in these teachings. Today, in the twentieth century, millions of Bahá'ís live their lives so that they can demonstrate these teachings and bring them to all people, everywhere.

In the *Golden Crowns* series, Lowell Johnson tells the stories of some of these early believers who won the crown of martyrdom. One of these believers was Ṭáhirih. Ṭáhirih's story now follows.

* Bahá'u'lláh appointed His eldest Son, 'Abdu'l-Bahá, as the Centre of the Covenant. He guided the Bahá'ís until He passed away in Haifa, Israel, on the 28th of November 1921. ''Abdu'l-Bahá' means the 'Servant of Bahá' or the 'Servant of the Glory'.

# Note

*For this edition, these stories have
been extensively revised. They may
be read aloud effectively, or else
used for private reading.*

# Ṭáhirih

'Ṭáhirih', meaning the 'Pure One', is the title given to the first woman believer in the Báb. The title was given to her by Bahá'u'lláh, and later confirmed by the Báb. You will see why she was called the 'Pure One', as we tell the story of Ṭáhirih.

Ṭáhirih was born in Qazvín, Írán (Persia) in 1817, the same year in which Bahá'u'lláh was born. Qazvín is a city which at that time was one of the main centres of the Muslim religion. Her father was a priest and a teacher, a very famous and intelligent clergyman in Írán. Her father's brother was also a priest and just as well known. Ṭáhirih's brother was very much like his father, so the three men were always discussing religion in the home. Ṭáhirih, therefore, heard much about religion from the day she was born.

Ṭáhirih was not like most children who would rather play than study their books. She passed most of her time listening to her parents and family talk about God and the Muslim religion. As they talked, she learned many things, and part of what she learned was this: her family was confused about religion, and didn't really understand its spiritual meaning. When she discovered this, she began to study religion for herself.

Even as a child, she became very well known in Qazvín as a prodigy, a person who is more intelligent and clever than most. When she was born, she was named Fáṭimih Umm-Salamih, but she was never called by that name. She was such an outstanding child that the family always called her 'Zarrín-Táj', which means 'Crown of Gold'. When her father taught his classes in religion, there would be hundreds of men studying, but no women. Women were treated only like animals in those days, especially in that part of the world. The men believed that they were good only for doing the housework and bearing the children. In public, the women always had to wear a veil.

But young Zarrín-Táj received permission from her father to

listen to him teach his classes. He told her she could listen, but that she must always sit behind a curtain so that none of the men would know she was there. Zarrín-Táj's father once said that he wished his daughter were a son, because if she were his son she would follow in her father's footsteps and add glory to the family name. Little did he know what glory she would add to his name in the future.

Little Zarrín-Táj was happy to listen to her father's lectures from behind the curtain. But sometimes she could not remain completely quiet. One day she became so excited by what her father was saying that, without thinking, she spoke up from behind the curtain and told her father that he had made a mistake in what he had just said. Her father was very surprised, and quite angry, as well. But Zarrín-Táj proved that he was wrong in what he had just said, and from then on everyone knew that she was behind the curtain. She was even permitted to take part in all the discussions.

At the age of thirteen, Zarrín-Táj was married to a cousin, Mullá Muḥammad. Her parents arranged the marriage, as that was the custom. Mullá Muḥammad was not her choice for a husband. But she lived with him for a while, and bore him three children. But most of the time she spent at the home of her father and mother, until she became a follower of Siyyid Káẓim and left the city of Qazvín.

Now, this is how Zarrín-Táj learned of Siyyid Káẓim. One day, she was visiting the home of a cousin. Wherever she went she was always interested in what books people were reading, and what books they had in their libraries. In this cousin's home, she saw some books written by two great scholars, Shaykh Aḥmad and Siyyid Káẓim. She looked through them, and asked if she could take them home with her. The cousin told her that her father would not like her to read those books, because they were written by very modern thinkers. These books did not agree with the way her father taught the Muslim religion. This pleased Zarrín-Táj very much, because she did not agree with her father, either. So, she promised to take good care of the books, and her cousin let her have them.

In one of these books, she read that the time was soon to come

As a child, Ṭáhirih learned much about religion.

when a new Prophet of God would appear Who would fulfil all the promises of all the religions, and especially the promises made by Muḥammad in the Holy Qur'án. The book was so logical and convincing that Zarrín-Táj longed to meet these teachers. But, Shaykh Aḥmad had passed on a few years before, and Siyyid Káẓim was living a long way away in Karbilá in the country of 'Iráq. And in those countries it was not permitted for a woman to travel alone.

Zarrín-Táj became more and more interested in this new teaching of Shaykh Aḥmad and Siyyid Káẓim though, and she told everyone about it. Her family and her husband became very angry with her, but she could think only of the new Teacher Who was to come into the world. She even told her uncle that she wanted to be the first woman to serve the new Prophet when He appeared, because she knew how low Írán had sunk and how poorly educated the women were and she wanted to help them. She said to her uncle, 'Oh, when will the day come when new laws will be revealed on the earth? I shall be the first to follow these new Teachings and give my life for my sisters!'

Zarrín-Táj tried to discuss these new teachings with her father, but he would not listen. Therefore, she wrote letters to Siyyid Káẓim himself, to ask him the many questions she had in her mind. Siyyid Káẓim answered all her questions so well that Zarrín-Táj began to admire him more and more. She was so pleased with his answers that she wrote a long paper praising the teachings of Shaykh Aḥmad and defending these teachings against the many people who tried to prove that they were wrong. This paper was so intelligent, and it explained the teachings of Shaykh Aḥmad so simply that Siyyid Káẓim wrote her a letter which started with these words: 'O thou who art the solace of mine eyes, and the joy of my heart!' In Persian, the words 'solace of my eyes' are translated 'Qurratu'l-'Ayn'—and from then on Zarrín-Táj became known by the name Qurratu'l-'Ayn.

## 2

After Qurratu'l-'Ayn had received her letter from Siyyid Kázim, she decided she must go to Karbilá to see him. But, what excuse could she use? Her father would never give his permission for her to visit Siyyid Kázim. And certainly he would never permit her to travel hundreds of kilometres across the desert alone. But Qurratu'l-'Ayn thought of a plan.

Karbilá is one of the holy cities in the religion of Islám. Many people go there every year to visit the shrines—if they cannot go to Mecca and Medina. Qurratu'l-'Ayn had always wanted to visit these shrines, although being a woman, she was not expected to do so. However, she talked to her sister, and they decided they must ask their father's permission to visit the shrines in Karbilá. Her father knew that if she went to Karbilá, she would also visit Siyyid Kázim. But he decided that he would let her go anyway. He hoped that seeing the sacred shrines of Islám would make her change her mind, and that she would become a true Muslim again.

The journey to Karbilá was made in 1843. Qurratu'l-'Ayn was twenty-six years old at that time, and the mother of two sons and one daughter. She had already become famous all over Írán as the most beautiful and the most educated woman in the country. It would be a wonderful to have a picture of this great woman of Írán, but no photos of her were ever taken, and no artists ever painted her while she was alive. Therefore, the only picture we can have of her is a spiritual one.

After making the long journey from Qazvín to Karbilá, Qurratu'l-'Ayn went straight to the home of Siyyid Kázim. But when she arrived, she received a great disappointment. Siyyid Kázim had passed from this world only ten days before. She was overcome with sadness and wept for many days. So disappointed was she about not meeting her new teacher that Siyyid Kázim's family invited her to stay with them. They let her read all of his writings, many of which had never been published. She studied them eagerly, and even taught some of Siyyid Kázim's students. When she was teaching, she would sit behind a curtain, as she had done in Qazvín when she was in her father's classes. It must have seemed very strange for Siyyid Kázim's students, who were all men, to hear the voice of a woman teaching them from behind a thick curtain.

# 3

Qurratu'l-'Ayn stayed for three years in Karbilá. But during this time many things happened. One of the most important things was this: One night, after she had kept the fast and meditated during the day, she had a dream. In this dream, she saw a young Man, a descendant of the Prophet Muḥammad, in the heavens. This young Man was standing in the air, repeating certain words and praying. Qurratu'l-'Ayn remembered some of these words and wrote them down when she awoke.

In a few days' time, she learned that her sister's husband, Mírzá Muḥammad 'Alí, was soon to leave Qazvín in search of the Promised One. As soon as she heard the news, Qurratu'l-'Ayn sent a sealed letter to him and asked him to deliver it to the Promised One when he found Him. She said, 'You are sure to meet the Promised One in the course of your journey. Say to Him from me, "The light of Thy face flashed before my eyes, and its rays arose high above me. Then speak the word, 'Am I not your Lord?' and 'Thou art, Thou art!' we will all reply." '

Mírzá Muḥammad 'Alí took Qurratu'l-'Ayn's letter with him on his journey. When he recognized the Báb in S̲h̲íráz, he became the sixteenth Letter of the Living.* At the same time, he gave to the Báb the letter and the message from Qurratu'l-'Ayn. When the Báb read it, He immediately declared her the seventeenth Letter of the Living. And so, Qurratu'l-'Ayn was the only one of the Letters of

* The first eighteen people to recognize the Báb were called 'Letters of the Living'.

the Living who never came into the presence of the Báb, but through her dream she had recognized Him!

When Mullá 'Alí, the fourth Letter of the Living, left Shíráz, he received instructions from the Báb to take the news of the Faith to Karbilá. The Báb sent some of His Arabic Writings with Mullá 'Alí, and when Qurratu'l-'Ayn read these Writings, she found in them the words she had heard in her dream, and which she had written down. She was sure, then, that the Báb in Shíráz was the same man she had seen in her dream.

So hungry was Qurratu'l-'Ayn for news about the Báb that she kept Mullá 'Alí with her for a long, long time, asking him questions. She would not let him rest until she knew everything. She studied the Writings of the Báb over and over, and then she began to translate the Books into Persian. She also wrote her own books and poems in Persian about the Báb and His Teachings.

# 4

Qurratu'l-'Ayn was not alone in Karbilá. With her were some women who may interest you. There were the mother and sister of Mullá Ḥusayn,* and a woman known as Shams-i-Ḍuḥá† which means the 'Morning Sun'. Shams-i-Ḍuḥá's real name was Khurshíd Bagum, but most people didn't use it. She later became the grand-mother of Mírzá Jalál who married 'Abdu'l-Bahá's daughter, Rúḥá Khánum.

Soon everyone in Karbilá knew that Qurratu'l-'Ayn had become a believer in the Báb, and that she was openly teaching His Faith in the Holy City of Islám itself. Not only did she teach this Faith, but she refused to celebrate the holy days of the Muslim religion any more. On the anniversary of the martyrdom of Ḥusayn (a very holy day in the Muslim religion), Qurratu'l-'Ayn asked her sister and her relatives to put away the black clothes usually worn on that day, and instead to wear bright, colourful dresses. Why? Because it was also

* See the booklet about Mullá Ḥusayn.          † Pronounced *Shams-seh-Ẓoha*.

the anniversary of the Birth of the Báb, and that was a day for great happiness and joy, not a day for wearing black!

When the priests of Karbilá heard about what Qurratu'l-'Ayn had done on such a holy day to Islám, they reported her actions to the Government and demanded that she be brought before the Governor of the city and punished. The government officials who were searching for her arrested Shams-i-Duhá by mistake. When Qurratu'l-'Ayn learned of this, she wrote to the Governor and told him that they had arrested the wrong woman. They must come and take her instead. The Governor became quite disgusted with these women and ordered a guard to keep Qurratu'l-'Ayn in her house. For three months she was not permitted to see anyone. No one was able to enter the house, and she was not permitted to leave.

Soon, Qurratu'l-'Ayn received the news that the Báb had called a conference of the leading Bábís in the province of Khurásán in Írán. Qurratu'l-'Ayn was gloriously happy! But she was a prisoner in her own home: how was she going to attend? Nothing was going to stop her from attending this conference, so she wrote a letter to the Governor and told him that she was leaving Karbilá for Baghdád. Baghdád was still in 'Iráq, but nearer the Iranian border, and therefore on her way to the conference.

The priests of Karbilá tried to stop Qurratu'l-'Ayn from leaving the city. They told her that the journey to Baghdád was too difficult and dangerous at this time. The real reason why they wanted her to stay in Karbilá was that the Governor had not yet announced what he was going to do with her for celebrating the birth of the Báb, instead of commemorating the Muslim holy day. They were still hoping that she would be publicly punished.

Naturally, their arguments had no effect on Qurratu'l-'Ayn. Instead, she wrote a long letter to each one of them telling them why she was going, and that she was quite able to make the journey— because there are no dangers when doing the will of God!

Soon she received permission from the Governor to leave Karbilá. But, he said, she must stay in Baghdád until a final decision was reached about her. The ladies packed their belongings and, with several men to protect them, they left for Baghdád. One of these companions was Mírzá Muḥammad 'Alí, the sixteenth Letter of the Living who had delivered her message to the Báb. As they were leaving the city, Qurratu'l-'Ayn was hit several times by stones which people threw at her.

When they arrived in Baghdád, Qurratu'l-'Ayn began to teach the Cause every day. People who had known her in the past came to listen to her lectures, and they were surprised at her power and her strength of words. 'This is not the woman we knew before', they would say. Her lectures attracted large crowds, and many people began to investigate the Truth for themselves, especially the women. Within a short time, many of her former students, both men and women, left Karbilá and came to Baghdád to attend her classes. Such was her power of attraction.

Here in Baghdád, just as in Karbilá, she invited the priests to come to a public discussion of these new religious teachings. The priests all made excuses, however, and refused to come. Instead they made a loud outcry against her, such a huge outcry that it reached the ears of the Government. To protect them, the Governor sent all the ladies to live in the house of the Judge of Baghdád.

Ṭáhirih and the other ladies lived with the Judge for some time, and the Judge was very impressed with their spirit. A few years later, when he wrote a book about his life experiences, he mentioned Qurratu'l-'Ayn's time in his home. He wrote that every morning in the early dawn she would arise and pray and meditate. Very often she would also fast. He added that he had never seen a woman more pure, nor one who had more knowledge. No woman was more brave or more eager to give her life to a cause. At one time he said of her, 'I see in her such knowledge, education, politeness, and good character as I have not seen in any great man in this century.'

It was 1847, and for three months she stayed in the home of the Judge. All this time she was waiting for her instructions. One day, the Judge brought her a message from the Governor. He said, 'You are

The city streets as Ṭáhirih saw them.

now free, but you must leave 'Iráq tomorrow. You must arrange
your things for travelling to Írán, for the Sulṭán commands it.' This
made Qurratu'l-'Ayn very happy, as she was eager to be on her
way to the conference in the province of Khurásán.

## 5

When Qurratu'l-'Ayn made her preparations for the journey back
to her home country, she found that more than thirty of her friends
wanted to go with her. Some were from 'Iráq and some were friends
who had come to her from Írán. She obtained permission for them
to go with her, and the Judge sent along ten horsemen under the
command of a general to protect them on their way. In this royal
manner, they left on their journey and in a few days' time they
reached the border of Írán. From there, they continued on their way
alone, without the horsemen, to the city of Kirmánsháh. On the way
to Kirmánsháh, they stayed for three days in the village of Karand.
Before leaving Karand, twelve hundred persons volunteered to
follow Qurratu'l-'Ayn and do her bidding.

In Kirmánsháh the men in the group stayed in one house and the
women in another. As soon as the people of the city learned that
Qurratu'l-'Ayn was there, they rushed to her house to see her. Even
princes, priests and government officials hurried to visit her. They
listened to her speeches and were impressed by her knowledge, her
power, and her beautiful character. She seemed to have no sense of
fear. She read the Writings of the Báb to everyone who came, and
answered everyone's questions. Even the wife of the Governor was
among the ladies who heard her speak, and when the Governor
himself heard her explain the Message of the Báb, he accepted the
Cause and told everyone how much he loved and admired Qurratu'l-
'Ayn.

But some of the priests of Kirmánsháh were not as friendly as the
Governor and the princes. The priests went to the Mayor of the city
and made some reports that were not true. The Mayor then had the

Bábís thrown out of the city. He even permitted a mob to attack their houses and steal everything that the Bábís owned. Then they were put into a wagon drawn by horses, and they were driven out into the desert. There, they were put out of the wagon, and left with no food, no change of clothing, and no blankets or rugs. It was very cold.

Qurratu'l-'Ayn wrote a letter to the Governor of Kirmánsháh, and explained to him what the Mayor had done. 'We were your guests in Kirmánsháh', she said. 'Do you think it was kind to treat us like this?' One of the group walked to Kirmánsháh to carry the message. When the Governor received the letter, he was very surprised, for he had known nothing about the order. He invited the whole group to return to Kirmánsháh as his guests, but this Qurratu'l-'Ayn refused to do. She was eager to go on to the conference being called by the Báb.

When the group reached the village of Hamadán, Qurratu'l-'Ayn was met by her brothers from Qazvín who delivered a message to her from her father. Her father wanted her to come home for a visit and stay for a while. She did not want to go, but she agreed because it was her father's desire. Before she left Hamadán, she asked some of her followers to go back to 'Iráq; she left others in Hamadán. Only a few of her companions went with her. Two of them were Shaykh Şálih and Mullá Ibráhím, both of whom soon died as martyrs, one in Ţihrán and one in Qazvín. Others were Shams-i-Duhá, Mírzá Muhammad-'Alí the Letter of the Living, and Siyyid 'Abdu'l-Hádí, who was promised in marriage to Qurratu'l-'Ayn's daughter. These last two had travelled with her all the way from Karbilá.

# 6

When Qurratu'l-'Ayn arrived at her father's home, a family discussion was held which included her father, her husband, and her uncle, who was also her father-in-law. When she told her family that she had completely given her love to the Teachings of the Báb, her father became very excited and showed her how really great he thought she was. He said to her: 'If you, with all the learning and intelligence you have, were to claim to be the Báb or even more than that, I would immediately agree with you and believe in you—but what can I do, when you choose to follow this young man from Shíráz?'

Qurratu'l-'Ayn answered her father: 'With the knowledge which I have, it is impossible that I could be mistaken in recognizing Him Who is the Lord of the worlds, Him Whom all the people are waiting for. I have recognized Him by the proofs of reason and the facts of knowledge. But this knowledge of mine is only a drop, compared with the great ocean of knowledge which is the Báb's.'

Her father was greatly impressed, but he could not see beyond his own daughter. He said, 'If you had been my son instead of my daughter, and if you had made the claim that you were the Báb yourself, I would have believed it.'

Qurratu'l-'Ayn's uncle, Mullá Taqí, became very angry during the evening, and cursed the Báb. In his anger he lost his temper and even hit Qurratu'l-'Ayn several times. She remained very calm, but she turned to him and said these prophetic words: 'O Uncle, I see your mouth filling with blood.'

The next day, her husband sent several ladies to her with the message that she must come back and live with him. Qurratu'l-'Ayn was not interested in living with her husband any more, because they no longer had anything in common. She said to the ladies, 'Tell my proud and false-hearted husband, "If you had really wanted to be a faithful husband and companion to me, you would have hurried to see me in Karbilá, and would have guided my carriage on foot all the way back to your home. If you had done that, I would have awakened you from your sleep of heedlessness while we travelled, and shown you the way to Truth. But this was not meant to be. We have been apart for three years. Neither in this world nor in the next can I ever again be with you. I have put you out of my life forever." '

So strong and final was her answer to her husband that he and his father became furiously angry. They immediately tried to prove that she was a bad woman, and that everything she told the people was untrue. Qurratu'l-'Ayn was quite able to defend herself in every way, and she proved by her actions that it was not her character which was poor, but her husband's.

Qurratu'l-'Ayn's father was a peaceful, fair-minded man. He tried to bring his daughter and husband together again, but it was no use. A few weeks later, her husband divorced her.

It was during this difficult time that a certain Mullá 'Abdu'lláh committed a murder in Qazvín, which caused great trouble to Qurratu'l-'Ayn. Mullá 'Abdu'lláh killed Mullá Taqí, Qurratu'l-'Ayn's uncle, because Mullá Taqí had ordered the persecution and death of Mullá Ibráhím, one of Qurratu'l-'Ayn's recent companions on her journey. This murder filled the family of Mullá Taqí with even more hate and anger against Qurratu'l-'Ayn. They claimed that she had given the order for his death. You will remember that she said to Mullá Taqí on the night of the family conference, 'O Uncle, I see your mouth filling with blood.' This news got around the family, and they said, 'No one else but you is guilty of the murder of our father. You gave the order that he must be killed.'

Of course, what they said was not true. But, nevertheless, the family succeeded in having her placed under strict guard in her own father's home. The women who were chosen to watch over her were ordered not to let her out of her room, except for the purpose of washing herself once a day.

Many of the other Bábís were arrested after this murder was committed. The clergy found it a convenient time to get rid of as many Bábís as they could. Therefore, the entire company of Bábís was sent to the prison in the capital city, Ṭihrán. But Mullá Taqí's family was not satisfied that they should only be put in prison. They wanted them all killed, because one of them had killed their father.

The case was then brought before the King himself, and he gave the order that only the murderer could be killed—the others must be released. The family could not find the real murderer, as he was hiding somewhere. Therefore, they declared another Bábí, Shaykh Ṣáliḥ, to be the murderer. You will remember that he came with Qurratu'l-'Ayn on the journey to her home.

Shaykh Ṣáliḥ was arrested and told that he was to die for the murder of Mullá Taqí. As he was brought to the place where he was to be hanged, his face was filled with joy. He was not afraid to die. He was happy. He hurried to greet the man who was to kill him, as though he were a dear and lifelong friend. Just before he was killed, he spoke beautifully of the Báb, and said, 'I gave up the hopes and the beliefs of men from the moment I recognized Thee, Thou Who art my Hope and my Belief!' Shaykh Ṣáliḥ was buried in the court-yard of one of the Muslim shrines in Ṭihrán.

The death of Shaykh Ṣáliḥ did not satisfy Mullá Taqí's family. When the innocent Bábís were returned to Qazvín, all of them were put to death. A mob of men carrying knives, swords, spears, and axes attacked the defenceless Bábís, and cut them to pieces. The bits of their bodies were thrown in so many different directions that it was not possible to find any part of them for a proper burial. All this was done in the name of Muḥammad, in the city of Qazvín, where no less than a hundred of the highest leaders of the Muslim religion had their homes and lived their lives!

And still the family of Mullá Taqí were not satisfied. They next turned their attention to Qurratu'l-'Ayn herself. They insisted that she must suffer the same kind of death as had all the rest.

During all this trouble, Mullá Muḥammad, Qurratu'l-'Ayn's husband, had been following in his father's footsteps and become the highest religious leader in Qazvín. When Qurratu'l-'Ayn learned that her enemies were going to kill her too, she wrote a letter to her husband, and this is what she said: 'If my Cause be the Cause of Truth, if the Lord whom I worship be none other than the one true God, He will deliver me from this house before nine days have passed. If God does not deliver me from here you are free to do what you wish with me.'

In some way, Bahá'u'lláh learned of Qurratu'l-'Ayn's danger and her brave announcement to her husband. He immediately sent Muḥammad-Hádí, Qurratu'l-'Ayn's eldest brother, to Qazvín to help her escape. Bahá'u'lláh gave him a letter which he was to give to his wife, Khátún-Ján, to deliver to Qurratu'l-'Ayn.

Khátún-Ján was a faithful friend of Qurratu'l-'Ayn, and the only person who could see her while she was kept in her father's house. She found many excuses to go to visit her sister-in-law. Sometimes she would go there pretending that she must wash some clothes—any excuse was used. In this way, she would carry food, and help Qurratu'l-'Ayn through her difficult times.

Bahá'u'lláh instructed Khátún-Ján to go to Qurratu'l-'Ayn's house in the clothes of a beggar. She must deliver the letter into her own hands, wait at the entrance of the house until Qurratu'l-'Ayn joined her, and then hurry to Muḥammad-Hádí.

Then, He told Muḥammad-Hádí that, as soon as Qurratu'l-'Ayn had joined him, he must start immediately for Ṭihrán. That very night, Bahá'u'lláh would send someone to Qazvín with three horses. Muḥammad-Hádí must bring Qurratu'l-'Ayn to a spot outside the city walls, climb on the horses, and try to get to Ṭihrán before daybreak. As soon as the gates of the city were opened, they must come immediately to Bahá'u'lláh's house. Bahá'u'lláh said he must be very careful that no one could recognize who she is. Then He added: 'The Almighty will assuredly guide your steps and surround you with His unfailing protection.'

Everything was done as Bahá'u'lláh had commanded. When Qurratu'l-'Ayn read the letter, she said to Khátún-Ján, 'You go, and I shall follow.' Within the hour, she was on her way. They took her to the house of a carpenter where no one would look for her. From there they climbed over the city wall, and went to a slaughter-house where the horses were waiting. With no trouble at all, they reached the city of Ṭihrán, and, at the proper time, found themselves in the home of Bahá'u'lláh.

As you can see, nine days had not yet gone by before Qurratu'l-

'Ayn was delivered from the danger in Qazvín. The city of Qazvín
was shocked. The whole night they searched the houses for Qurratu'l-
'Ayn. The house belonging to <u>Kh</u>átún-Ján's father was robbed of all
its goods. Her promise to be out of the hands of her guards within
nine days had surprised everyone. As a result of what had happened,
a few people came to realize the greatness of the Faith she had
accepted, and some of them became followers of the Báb.

# 7

When Qurratu'l-'Ayn entered the house of Bahá'u'lláh, she knew
full well Who Bahá'u'lláh was, and what He was going to be. She
had recognized the Báb without even seeing Him, and it was this
same spiritual greatness that caused her to recognize the future glory
of Bahá'u'lláh. Even in the year 1844, while she was in Karbilá, she
had written poems which clearly showed that she knew that both the
Báb and Bahá'u'lláh were Prophets of God. Nothing else could have
given her the courage to do the things which she did during the next
few months of her life.

At this time, 'Abdu'l-Bahá was a little boy only three or four
years old. One day, the great scholar Vaḥíd* came to visit Qurratu'l-
'Ayn. Vaḥíd was one of the early believers who was later martyred
in Nayríz. He waited for a long time to see her. But Qurratu'l-'Ayn
was at that moment holding 'Abdu'l-Bahá on her lap, as she so often
did. Quite a long time went by, and Qurratu'l-'Ayn made no move
to go and talk to the great Vaḥíd. One of the women in the house
became worried, and she said, 'Shouldn't you leave the child now,
and go to speak with Vaḥíd?' But Qurratu'l-'Ayn pulled little
'Abdu'l-Bahá even closer to her and said, 'Shall I leave Thee,
Protector of the Cause, to go and see one of the followers of the
Cause?'

Those who heard her say this were greatly surprised, for no one
knew what she meant. Today, although no one knows if it is true,

* See the booklet on Vaḥíd, to be published.

some people believe that Bahá'u'lláh had told her many things about what the future would be, and especially about the importance of 'Abdu'l-Bahá as the protector of Bahá'u'lláh against His enemies in the many years to come.

A few days after Qurratu'l-'Ayn arrived in Ṭihrán, Bahá'u'lláh decided to send her on to <u>Kh</u>urásán. The long-awaited conference called by the Báb was about to begin. Bahá'u'lláh Himself was to follow her in a few days' time. He, therefore, called His own brother, Áqáy-i-Kalím, into His presence and gave him instructions about Qurratu'l-'Ayn's journey. He told Áqáy-i-Kalím that he must be very careful as he took Qurratu'l-'Ayn through the gates of the city, as the guards had been given orders not to allow any women to pass through. If they discovered who Qurratu'l-'Ayn was, they would not let her leave.

Áqáy-i-Kalím was very careful to follow all of Bahá'u'lláh's instructions. He and Qurratu'l-'Ayn put their trust in God, and when they came to the gate, none of the guards took any notice of them. They rode out of the city safely and easily, and they did not stop riding for several kilometres.

After two hours of riding, they came to a lovely orchard of trees situated at the foot of a mountain. In the centre of this orchard was a house which looked as though no one lived in it. As Áqáy-i-Kalím went looking for someone who might be in charge of the house, he came across an old man watering some plants. Áqáy-i-Kalím asked the old man, 'Where are the owners of this house?' and the old man said, 'The owners are not here. There has been an argument over who owns this place, and until the problem is settled, I have been asked to watch over it.'

Áqáy-i-Kalím was very happy to hear this news, because it meant that Qurratu'l-'Ayn would be safe for a while in this place. They invited the old man to share their lunch with them, and then Áqáy-i-Kalím asked the old man if he would take care of Qurratu'l-'Ayn for a few hours while he made arrangements for their journey to <u>Kh</u>urásán. The old man agreed, and all was settled.

When Áqáy-i-Kalím left Qurratu'l-'Ayn, he went back into Ṭihrán through the same gates to tell Bahá'u'lláh what had happened, and he sent Mullá Báqir, one of the Letters of the Living, to join Qurratu'l-'Ayn at the house in the orchard. Bahá'u'lláh was greatly pleased that everything had worked out so well, and He named the orchard the 'Garden of Paradise'. Then He said, 'That house has been prepared by the Almighty for this purpose, so that you may entertain in it the loved ones of God.'

Qurratu'l-'Ayn stayed in that house for seven days. Then she set out with several others for the great conference called by the Báb.

# 8

The conference called by the Báb in the province of Khurásán was held in the little village of Badasht. Badasht lies between Ṭihrán and Mázindarán. It was an out-of-the-way summer place full of gardens and grassland with only a few houses. It was the perfect place to hold a private conference. It would have been too dangerous to hold such a gathering in Ṭihrán. Bahá'u'lláh had selected Badasht, because it was quiet.

It was the beginning of summer. When Bahá'u'lláh arrived in Badasht, He rented three gardens. One was for Quddús, the leader of the Bábís.* The second was for Qurratu'l-'Ayn and her servant, and the third was for Himself. In the middle of these three gardens there was an open place like a court. There, the believers could consult comfortably and freely.

The Báb was not able to attend, because He was in prison.

Those who gathered in Badasht for this very first conference of the New Age were eighty-one in number. Every day, Bahá'u'lláh revealed a new Tablet, or explanation, which one of the Bábís would chant for everyone to hear. In these Tablets, He gave each person present a new name for the New Day. He Himself accepted the name 'Bahá', which the Báb had already given to Him. And to

* See the booklet about Quddús.

Qurratu'l-'Ayn He gave the title 'Ṭáhirih'. Ṭáhirih, you remember, means the 'Pure One'. At a later time during the conference, when Ṭáhirih did some things which to some of the believers did not seem to be very pure, they questioned whether Bahá'u'lláh had given her the right name. But later, when the Báb learned that some of the men were doubting Bahá'u'lláh's wisdom, He wrote to them from His prison: 'What am I to say regarding her whom the Tongue of Power and Glory has named Ṭáhirih?' In other words, the Báb made it clear that He did not question the wisdom of Bahá'u'lláh and that He agreed with the name given to her. From then on Qurratu'l-'Ayn was known as Ṭáhirih.

Many of the men present at this conference wondered why Ṭáhirih, a woman, was permitted to consult with the men, even from behind a curtain. When one of them questioned her about it, she answered, 'Our talk is about God, about religion, about spiritual matters, and above all, about giving our lives in the path of Truth. Know that every step we take is in the path of God. Are you prepared to follow us?'

At this time in the development of the Cause, the Báb had not yet revealed to His followers His full importance. He had declared Himself to be the Báb (the Gate), but He had not yet told them that He was the beginning of a whole new era, and that laws would necessarily have to be changed. It was left to Bahá'u'lláh, Ṭáhirih and Quddús to prepare the rest of the believers to accept these new, revolutionary ideas.

Then, on a certain day, Bahá'u'lláh was ill and stayed in His tent —and indeed there was a wisdom in this. Quddús came out of his own garden and went immediately to see Bahá'u'lláh. Soon, the others gathered around Bahá'u'lláh's tent—all the believers, except Ṭáhirih. Being a woman, she was not permitted to be in the presence of the men, unless she stayed behind a curtain where no one could see her.

While everyone was gathered around Bahá'u'lláh, Ṭáhirih sent a message to Quddús to come to see her in her garden. Quddús refused to go. This did not surprise anyone, but what happened next surprised everyone. Because Quddús would not come to see her, she came to see him! And not only did she come into the garden of Bahá'u'lláh where all the men were—but she came without her veil, and beautifully dressed! Quietly, silently, and with the greatest calm and dignity, Ṭáhirih stepped forward and seated herself beside Quddús.

Such a thing had never been seen by any man before. Everyone was afraid, angry, and confused to the depths of their souls. One man was so shocked that he cut his own throat and ran away from the face of Ṭáhirih. Many others followed him, and the rest stood speechless before her. In the meantime, Quddús remained seated in his place, but his face was very angry. It seemed that at any moment he would lift the sword in his hand and kill her.

But his anger did not affect Ṭáhirih in the least. Her face was filled with a feeling of joy and triumph. She rose to her feet and, paying no attention to the fear and anger of her companions, she began to talk to them in words which sounded very much like the style of the Qur'án. She was a poetess, and she had never used more beautiful words. She finished her talk with a sentence from the Qur'án which reads, 'Verily, amid gardens and rivers shall the pious dwell in the seat of truth, in the presence of the potent King.'

Indeed, they were at that moment sitting in gardens beside rivers and, as she said it, she glanced at both Bahá'u'lláh and Quddús, so that no one could tell which one she meant was the King. Then she spoke the words, 'I am the Word which the Promised One is to speak, the Word which shall make the chiefs and the nobles of the earth afraid! The Trumpet is sounding! The great Trump is blown!' With these words, Ṭáhirih awakened sleeping souls. After she had spoken, Bahá'u'lláh had someone read the Súrih of the Inevitable from the Qur'án, which tells of the Day of Resurrection. This shows what an important moment that was: the Day of Resurrection had begun!

Ṭáhirih then turned her face toward Quddús and said, 'You were

Ṭáhirih announced the coming of the new Age.

not very careful about the way you served the Faith in K͟hurásán.'
Quddús answered, 'I can do as I think best. I do not have to follow
the will and the good-pleasure of my fellow disciples.' Ṭáhirih then
turned away from Quddús and spoke to the others. 'This is the day to
be happy', she said. 'It is the day when everything in the past is
forgotten. Let all of us who have shared this great occasion arise and
embrace each other.'

It seems a very important thing that a woman was chosen to
announce the new Age to the followers of the Báb. It showed, indeed,
that the new Age was to be completely different from the past. For
instance, women were to become equal with men, for the first time
in history. For a woman to be given the responsibility of announcing
the end of the old laws showed that a great revolution was about to
take place in all things.

But great changes bring about great tests. As the old laws were
thrown aside each day at the conference, most of the men became
more and more confused. A few men thought that it was wrong to
end the old laws, especially while the Báb was not there. Others
turned to Ṭáhirih and accepted her as the only person who could be
the judge in these matters. Others felt that Quddús was the proper
person to decide about such things, because he was considered to be
the true representative of the Báb at this meeting. A few believed that
both Quddús and Ṭáhirih were right, and that this conference was
meant to be a test of their faith.

The quarrel between Ṭáhirih and Quddús lasted for several days.
Ṭáhirih would say to the Bábís, 'Quddús has made many mistakes,
and I was sent here by the Báb to teach him what to do.' Quddús
would then answer, 'Ṭáhirih is the one who is really wrong. Anyone
who follows Ṭáhirih is walking down the wrong path.' After a few
days, Bahá'u'lláh stepped in and stopped the whole argument in His
wonderful way. He brought Ṭáhirih and Quddús together, and both
began to serve again in a constructive way.

The Conference of Badas͟ht lasted only twenty-two days. The
exciting discussions caught the attention of a number of the people

who lived nearby, and they soon attacked the Bábís and stole their possessions. The Conference broke up very suddenly.

After the Conference, Bahá'u'lláh and Ṭáhirih left for the village of Níyálá. There, Bahá'u'lláh was arrested by the Governor of Ámul because of all the trouble concerning the Bábís. Ṭáhirih was separated from Bahá'u'lláh, and taken under guard back to Ṭihrán where she was kept in the house of Maḥmúd Khán, the Mayor of Ṭihrán.

# 9

One day, Ṭáhirih was brought before the King, Náṣiri'd-Dín Sháh. When he saw her, he said 'I like her looks. Leave her, and let her be.' But Ṭáhirih was still kept at the home of the Mayor.

During her imprisonment, Ṭáhirih was at first kept in a little room where there were no stairs. A ladder had to be put up each time she came out or went in. One of the princesses of Írán, who was a poetess, came especially to walk past this house, hoping to see Ṭáhirih. She was rewarded with a glimpse of her as Ṭáhirih walked on her balcony. Later, in one of her books, she tells how completely happy Ṭáhirih was. No matter where we read about Ṭáhirih in history books and stories, we always hear of her as being happy—as being full of joy in her religion. She was always bright and enthusiastic, and even when in the greatest danger herself, she was always inspiring others with her courage. She was not only a martyr, she was a smiling, joyful, beautiful young woman.

It is also reported that the King sent a message to her in the care of the Mayor asking her to give up her belief in the Báb and become a true Muslim again. He said that if she would do this, he would make her his wife and she would be the guardian of all the ladies in the royal household. But Ṭáhirih wrote her reply in verse on the back of his letter, and returned it to him. In English, the message went something like this:

Kingdom, wealth and ruling be for thee,
Wandering, becoming a poor dervish and calamity be for me.

If that station is good, let it be for thee,
And if this station is bad, I long for it, let it be for me!

When the King read her reply, he spoke of her courage and
wonderful spirit, and said: 'So far, history has not shown such a
woman to us.'

One day there was a great gathering at the Mayor's home. It was
the day when the Mayor's son was getting married. Naturally
many fine ladies of the city were there—princesses, wives of ministers,
and other ladies of importance. The Mayor had gone to great
expense to have music and dancing and the best of entertainment.
During the entertainment, Ṭáhirih began to speak. The ladies
became so interested in what she had to say that they forgot all about
the music and the dancing, and spent the rest of the time listening to
the words of Ṭáhirih.

Not long after Ṭáhirih had come to live with the Mayor of Ṭihrán,
the ladies of the household grew to love her very much. They asked
permission for her to leave her little room with no stairs, and to live
with them in their own home. Ṭáhirih was given a lovely room with
a balcony on the second floor of the house, and although she was
still a prisoner and could not leave the house, she was allowed to
have any number of visitors.

Both men and women came to see her and talk with her in Ṭihrán.
For three years she lived like this in the house of the Mayor, and it
may be said that these three years were the most important ones in
her service to the Faith.

She talked to the women and showed them what a low place they
had in the Muslim religion, and how they would be given more
freedom and respect in the Bábí religion. Through her talks, many
women became Bábís.

This would have continued for many more years, but for the
attempt by a young man to kill the King. Many Bábís were wrongly
accused of having a part in this. The Premier ordered two priests
to visit Ṭáhirih and find out what she was teaching. These two priests
visited Ṭáhirih seven times. Each time Ṭáhirih talked with them and

Ṭáhirih prepared for her martyrdom.

insisted that the Báb was the promised Imám expected by the followers of Muḥammad. The priests tried to show her that the Báb could not be the Promised One because, according to the Muslim prophecies, the Imám was supposed to come from the cities of Jábulqá and Jábulsá—the Báb came from the city of Shíráz. Ṭáhirih answered that those prophecies had been forged by false writers, and that there were no such cities as Jábulqá and Jábulsá, and had never been any such cities—they could only be the superstitions of diseased brains. No matter how she explained the Teachings of the Báb, however, she always met with the same argument from the priests—the Promised One must come from the cities of Jábulqá and Jábulsá!

Finally, she lost her patience with these priests, and she said, 'Your reasoning is like that of an ignorant and stupid child. How long will you keep repeating these stupidities and lies? When will you lift your eyes toward the Sun of Truth?'

The priests were shocked by such a statement. They stood up and said, 'Why continue our discussion with a non-believer?' They returned home, and wrote out her sentence of death, in the name of the Holy Qur'án!

A relative of Ṭáhirih tells that the day before she was killed, she was called before the King and asked the question, 'Why should you be a believer in the Báb?' She replied with a sentence from the Qur'án which reads like this: 'I do not worship whom you worship, and you do not worship whom I worship. I shall never worship whom you worship, and you will never worship whom I worship. Therefore, permit that I worship whom I wish and you worship whom you wish.'

When he heard this verse from the Qur'án, the King bent his head in silence for a long time, and then he arose and walked out of the room without a word. The King did not give the order for Ṭáhirih to be killed. It was done the next day without his knowledge, and when he learned that the deed had been done, he was filled with sorrow and tears.

## 10

There are many stories about the death of Ṭáhirih. Not all of them agree upon the exact way in which she was killed. But all do agree that she knew beforehand that her time had come, that she prepared herself as a bride for the supreme moment, and that she met her murder bravely, without fear.

In one account, at the hour of her death, she said to a guard: 'You can kill me as soon as you like, but you cannot stop the emancipation of women.'

The story of her death which is likely to be most complete is the one told by the wife and the son of the Mayor, who were present with her on that last night.

It was the day after Ṭáhirih's visit to the King. The priests had secretly given the order that she must be killed. This order was passed on to the Mayor and to the police.

As the Mayor's son tells the story he says, 'On the day that she was secretly killed, it seemed as if she had been told it was going to happen. Ṭáhirih bathed, changed all of her clothing and came downstairs to see the family. One by one, she asked their pardon for having stayed in our house for so long, and for causing us so much trouble. She was like a traveller getting herself ready for a journey. She busied herself with the greatest pleasure and joy. Near sunset, as she usually did, she started walking back and forth on her balcony. She talked to no one, but she was quietly whispering to herself. This continued until three hours after sunset.

'In the evening, my father came to me and said: "I have made all the necessary arrangements, and I have commanded all the watchmen to be very awake tonight, in case anyone finds out about this order to kill Ṭáhirih and tries to stop it. Now, I want you to go with these guards and take Ṭáhirih to the police station. You must stay there until the case is settled, then you must come back and report to me, so that I may go and inform the King." '

The Mayor's wife loved Ṭáhirih very greatly, although she never became a follower of the Báb. Her story of Ṭáhirih's last night is this: 'That night, Ṭáhirih called me to her room. When I walked into the room, I saw that she was wearing a dress made of snow-white silk. Her room was filled with beautiful perfume. I was surprised to find her like this, so I asked her, "What is the reason for this dress and this perfume?" She answered, "I am preparing to meet my Beloved. I shall no longer be a prisoner in your home." I was shocked at the idea of her leaving us, and tears filled my eyes which I could not stop. Ṭáhirih tried to comfort me by saying, "You must not cry. The time for tears has not yet come. Listen to me. I want to share with you my last wishes, for the hour when I shall be arrested and killed is soon coming. This is my wish: I want you to let your son come with me to the place of my death so that he can protect me if the guards try to take off these clothes. I also want my body thrown into a pit and I want that pit filled with earth and stones. Three days after my death a woman will come to visit you. You must give her this parcel which I now deliver into your hands. My last wish is that you not allow anyone to come into my room until after I leave this house. No one must come to me while I am in my last prayers and devotions. This day I intend to fast—a fast which I shall not break until I am brought face to face with my Beloved."

'With these words, Ṭáhirih asked me to leave her room, to lock the door, and not to open it until the final hour. She also told me to keep the news of her coming death a secret, until her enemies should announce it themselves.

'I did as she had asked. I locked the door to her room and went to my own. I could not control my tears. I lay on my bed for hours, thinking of the great Ṭáhirih, and the end which was soon to come. I prayed, "Lord, Lord, turn from her, if it be Thy wish, the cup which her lips desire to drink."

'That day and night, I went quietly to her door and listened several times. Each time I heard her chanting prayers to her Beloved. The melody of her voice was so beautiful I could hardly remain

standing on my feet. Four hours after sunset, I heard a knocking at
the door. I went immediately to my son and told him of Ṭáhirih's
wishes. He gave his word that he would carry out every instruction
to the last detail. My son then went to the door and found the
guards standing at the gate. They demanded that Ṭáhirih be handed
over to them.

'I was filled with fear when I heard their voices. I walked slowly to
Ṭáhirih's room, unlocked the door, and found her veiled and ready
to leave. She was walking back and forth in her room chanting a
prayer of both sorrow and triumph. As soon as she saw me, she came
to me and kissed me. She put into my hands the key to her wardrobe
and said, "I have left a few little things in the wardrobe for you as a
remembrance of my stay in your house. Whenever you open it and
see the things I have left there, I hope you will remember me and be
happy in my gladness."

'With these words she said her last goodbye and left the house
with my son. As I stood by the door, I saw her climb on the horse
which the Chief of Police had sent for her to use. With my son and
a few guards, she rode out of my yard to the place of her martyrdom.'

Three hours later, her son returned to the house, his face covered
with tears and his mouth cursing the police and the guards. This is
the story he told.

'Mother, I can hardly describe what my eyes have seen tonight.
From our house, we went straight away to the Ílkhání garden,
outside the gate of the city. I went to the police office and reported to
the Chief of Police. He was there waiting for us, but he was drunk.
"Did anyone recognize you on the way?" he asked. I said, "No. No
one." He then called to a servant and said, "Take this handkerchief
and twist it around the neck of this Bábí woman, and choke her to
death. She is the cause of leading many people from the path of
Muḥammad." The servant left the room, and I went with him. He
went ahead and I stood by the door. When he came near to Ṭáhirih,
she looked at him and said a few words. He suddenly turned around
and came walking back. He was hanging his head and talking softly

to himself in Turkish. He walked out of the door, and did not come back.

'Ṭáhirih called to me and asked me to go to the Chief of Police with a special request. "It seems that they wish to strangle me", she said. "Long ago, I set aside a silk handkerchief which I hoped would be used for this purpose. I deliver it into your hands and I want you to ask that drunkard to use it for the purpose of taking my life."

'When I went to the Chief I found him completely drunk. He only shouted at me, "Don't interrupt our gay festival. Let that Bábí woman be strangled and her body thrown into a hole." I was greatly surprised by such an order, because it was exactly what she had wanted. I did not ask him whether he would permit the murderer to use the silk handkerchief. I just went to the two guards and they agreed that the handkerchief would be a good thing to use.

'A drunken servant was called and given the handkerchief. "You are such a brave man", the policeman said. "Can you choke this woman?" The servant said yes, and as soon as he reached Ṭáhirih, he quickly wrapped the silk handkerchief around her throat so tightly that she became unconscious and fell. It was a slow death. It seemed to take a long time. Finally, he kicked her in the side and the chest, and the deed was finished.

'I hurried to the gardener of this place, then, and asked whether he could suggest a spot where I could bury the body. He took me to a well which had been recently dug, and left unfinished. With the help of a few others, I lowered her into her grave and filled the well with earth and stones, as she had requested.'

And so ended the life of the glorious Ṭáhirih. On the third day after her martyrdom, a woman came to visit the wife of the Mayor. 'I asked her name,' said the Mayor's wife, 'and finding it to be the same as the one Ṭáhirih had told me, I delivered into her hands the parcel she had given to me. I had never before met that woman, nor did I ever see her again.'

The martyrdom of Ṭáhirih took place in August 1852. She was born in the year 1817, the same year as the birth of Bahá'u'lláh.

She was thirty-six years old when she suffered martyrdom in Ṭihrán. The time from the day she first heard of the coming of the Báb until the time she was martyred was a little less than nine years. Her career was as dazzling as it was short, as tragic as it was eventful. The lives of most of the early disciples of the Báb remain unknown to most of the world even to this day. But the life of Ṭáhirih quickly became famous, even as far as the capital cities of Europe. Both men and women of many nations, professions and cultures praised her, and admired her deeds and her sacrifice.

The world remembers Ṭáhirih as the first woman suffrage martyr. Bahá'ís remember her in the same way as other religions revere Sarah, Ásíyih, Fáṭimih, and the Virgin Mary. The call she put forth at the conference of Badasht and in Ṭihrán marked the end of the 1200-year-old law of Islám, and the beginning of a new era.

# Epilogue

Following are additional notes quoted from friends and historians about the importance of Ṭáhirih to the world.

As the news of Ṭáhirih's martyrdom quickly spread around the world, it reached the ears of the great actress Sarah Bernhardt who requested that a play be written for her about Ṭáhirih's life. Unfortunately, a suitable play has not yet been written.

One great Iranian Prince at the League of Nations in 1927 said, 'I was only a young man when I heard of the martyrdom of the gifted poetess Ṭáhirih in Ṭihrán, and I tell you, I wept for three days.'

Sulaymán Náẓim Big, a great author and poet of Turkey, wrote a book, *Náṣiri'd-Dín Sháh and the Bábís*. In it he closes his account of Ṭáhirih's life with the words: 'O Ṭáhirih, you are worth a thousand Náṣiri'd-Dín Sháhs!'

Mrs Marianna Hainisch of Vienna, Austria, mother of one of the Presidents of Austria, said in 1925: 'The greatest ideal of womanhood all my life has been Ṭáhirih (Qurratu'l-'Ayn) of Qazvín, Írán. I was only seventeen years old when I heard of her life and her martyrdom, but I said: "I shall try to do for the women of Austria what Țáhirih gave her life to do for women of Persia." ' No woman in Austria has done so much for freedom and education for women as has Mrs Marianna Hainisch.

Professor Edward G Browne, an English historian who was the only Westerner to meet Bahá'u'lláh in Person, had this to say about Țáhirih: 'The appearance of such a woman as Qurratu'l-'Ayn is, in any country and in any age, a rare phenomenon, but in such a country as Persia it is a prodigy—nay, almost a miracle. Alike in virtue of her marvellous beauty, her rare intellectual gifts, her fervid eloquence, her fearless devotion, and her glorious martyrdom, she stands incomparable and immortal amidst her countrywomen. Had the religion of the Báb no other claim to greatness, this were sufficient —that it produced a heroine like Qurratu'l-'Ayn.'

An account signed by Jináb-i-Adíb, a famous Bahá'í teacher who visited Bahá'u'lláh in 'Akká, has this to say: ' . . . in every meeting held in Țihrán, both women and men were speaking in Țáhirih's praise and honour. Many high-born, loving women came to her and were filled with joy because of her hopeful words. All were attracted by her eloquence, and people of all classes, even the royalty and ministers of state on entering her presence, humbly bowed before her. Her speeches and explanations were spread all over Írán, and no one had the least doubt about her erudition and scientific knowledge.

'While a youth I used to study philosophy with Mírzá 'Abdu'l-Vahháb, a brother of Țáhirih. When I had any doubts or made errors, I used to ask his help. One day in summer I went to him in his private court. He was alone and as it was a hot day he wore a loose, light garment. After sitting a little and finding a good oppor-tunity, I said: "I wanted to ask you some questions but I have hesitated. Now, if you will permit me, I shall ask you." He gave permission and I continued: "Both the learning and perfection of Țáhirih are so spread among the people that minds are amazed. No one knows better than you, and I want to know from you the truth or falsity of this matter."

'Then he sighed and responded: "You only hear the word of Ṭáhirih alas, you have not seen her! Know verily, that in a meeting where she sat neither I nor any one else could say a word. It was as if all the former and future books were with her. She used to explain a subject by bringing forth demonstrations and proofs from the learned books, page by page, so that no one had the power to deny. . . ."

'Since then the clergy have prevented all women from studying lest they should become believers like Ṭáhirih.'

With all these written records and these many praises and proofs of her greatness in the past, the true measure of her importance lies in her influence today. Nothing can show how deeply her sacrifice has penetrated the life of modern Írán more than this: When fathers in Írán today want to urge their daughters to progress, they say to them, 'Be a Ṭáhirih, be a Qurratu'l-'Ayn!'

# Sources

The following books were consulted in the writing of this story of Ṭáhirih:
'Abdu'l-Bahá, *Memorials of the Faithful* (Wilmette, 1971)
Bahá'u'lláh and 'Abdu'l-Bahá, *Bahá'í World Faith* (Wilmette 1956)
Shoghi Effendi, *God Passes By* (Wilmette, 1944)
J. E. Esslemont, *Bahá'u'lláh and the New Era* (London 1974 and Wilmette, 1950)
Nabíl, *The Dawn-Breakers* (Wilmette, 1932)
Martha L. Root, *Ṭáhirih the Pure, Írán's Greatest Woman* (Karachi, 1938)
All the quotations in the Epilogue are from *Ṭáhirih the Pure,* pages 84 and 85, except the one from Jináb-i-Adíb, which is on pages 69–71 of the same book.